Elliott Wa

Master Elliott Waves Techniques In Less Than 48 Hours

STEVE SINCLAIR

Legal & Disclaimer

The information contained in this book and its contents is not designed to replace or take the place of any form of medical or professional advice; and is not meant to replace the need for independent medical, financial, legal or other professional advice or services, as may be required. The content and information in this book have been provided for educational and entertainment purposes only.

The content and information contained in this book have been compiled from sources deemed reliable, and it is accurate to the best of the author's knowledge, information, and belief. However, the author cannot guarantee its accuracy and validity and cannot be held liable for any errors and/or omissions. Further, changes are periodically made to this book as and when needed. Where appropriate and/or necessary, you must consult a professional (including but not limited to your doctor, attorney, financial advisor or such other professional advisor) before using any of the suggested remedies, techniques, or information in this book.

Upon using the contents and information contained in this book, you agree to hold harmless the author from and against any damages, costs, and expenses, including any legal fees potentially resulting from the application of any of the information provided by this book. This disclaimer applies to any loss, damages or injury caused by the use and application, whether directly or indirectly, of any advice or information presented, whether for breach of contract, tort,

TABLE OF CONTENTS

INTRODUCTION

Elliott Wave theory has been used by almost all traders and investors in the financial markets. Whether you are a long-term trader or a scalper, it's always advisable to determine which wave you are in. With Elliott Wave, you have a powerful tool to help avoid the potential danger of trading against the primary trend.

The power of the Elliott Wave has gone beyond an analysis tool. It's not only a forecasting tool but also a full description of how the market behaves. In other words, by learning about the waves, you are able to read market price actions.

Born after a number of years studied and analyzed by his father - Ralph Nelson Elliot (1871-1948), the Elliott Wave is believed to work not only in the financial markets but also in social interaction and natural phenomena, just like the Fibonacci magical sequence. Basically, Elliott believed he discovered a powerful theory that could explain the behaviors of the crowd, exposing the momentums behind the ongoing swings between optimism and pessimism.

With its power, the Elliott Wave theory could be a perfect supplement to anyone who is struggling with trading with the trend. How many times have you failed to determine the trend correctly? How many times have you mistaken an impulsive move with a correction? Do you have difficulty making the most profit out of a large swing move?

With all the rules, tips, explanations, and examples presented in this book, you'll be able to find the solutions to all problems above. You'll understand how many phases or waves the price may experience, at which phase/wave the price is, what to expect in the next price movements, what to prepare before, during, and after the trade trigger. Also, this book is designed to suit both aggressive and conservative traders. You'll explore a number of waves and patterns in this book presented in a professional format so that you can refer any time you need. Last but not least, you will be exposed to a lot of trade illustrations to facilitate your learning curve.

Trading with Elliott Wave theory might seem complicated and time-consuming at first, but believe me, once you've got familiar with it, your trading will be enhanced immensely. You can avoid subjective decisions and self-destructive actions just by applying the wave count on any chart of assets. Think about it, if there is one tool preferred by many professional traders, it is definitely worth learning and applying.

Before we move into the main part, prepare a pen and some pieces of paper whether you are reading the kindle version or the print version. You might need them to help you grasp the most out of the knowledge presented in this book.

The best way to learn any strategy is to start at the beginning! My strategy is built around the Elliott Wave Theory, which is a near-century-old and proven strategy developed by the great Ralph Nelson Elliott. "R.N." as he was called, began his career as an accountant and, before his big discovery, he published two books: *Tea Room & Cafeteria Management* and *The Future of Latin America.*

After his visit to Central America, he contracted an illness that forced him to retire from accounting. He decided to spend the rest of his life studying the stock market. He started by analyzing huge amounts of market data. He examined 75 years of historical data of the DOW Index – from the yearly timeframe down to half-hour fluctuations.

His discovery was amazing. He managed to crack the market code without modern-day technology. Keep in mind that back then you needed to print charts by hand, and you didn't have access to any piece of code that could analyze the market. *So, everything R.N. Elliott did was manual!*

In all of the charts, he analyzed there were certain patterns that repeated themselves, and those same patterns repeated on a larger scale also. Today we know these patterns as "Elliott Waves".

In 1946 Elliott published his final work, **Nature's Law – The Secret of the Universe**, where he explained how the market works.

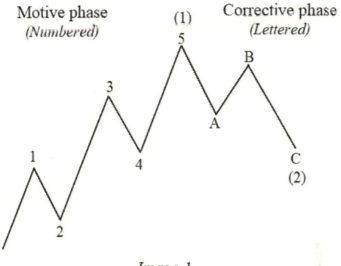

Image 1

Elliott discovered that the market has only two main phases that repeat, and you can see them on every single timeframe and in every single instrument. Image 1 above can illustrate this idea. The first phase is called the Motive Phase. This is the part of the cycle that moves in the direction of the larger trend. You will notice in Image 1 that the Motive Phase includes five waves labeled with numbers from 1 through 5. The second phase is called the Corrective Phase. This part of the cycle represents pullbacks that happen in the market. Within the Corrective Phase, we find three smaller waves labeled with the letters A, B, and C.

We know that the patterns repeat, so they link to each other and build the same pattern on a larger scale. The image below depicts an example of this.

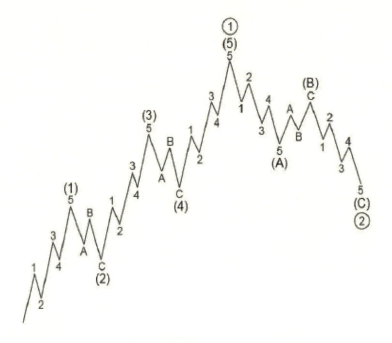

Image 2

Now, to make it simpler to grasp, let's suppose that Image 1 illustrates fluctuations on the 5-minute chart and that Image 2 represents the movements of the pair on the 15-minute chart.

We can advance now to see how these patterns would look on the largest scale.

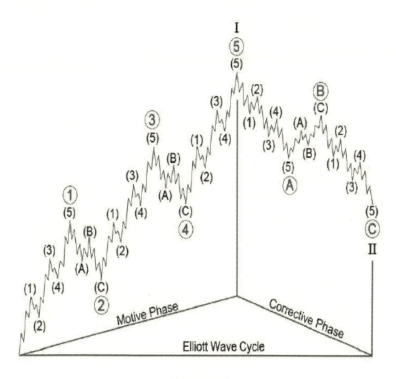

Image 3

In Image 3 we can see that we have much more waves, however, all need only to be counted from 1 to 5 and from A to C. True, you'll need to learn a few patterns and rules along the way, but I promise it's not that complicated at all.

Let's move to cover the first phase in the Elliott Wave Theory, The Motive Phase.

CHAPTER II: THE MOTIVE PHASE

The Motive Phase is the first group of patterns we need to learn in our quest to build a perfect trading strategy. In this group, we have just four different patterns to learn and most of the patterns have few things in common.

Each pattern from this group will have a five-wave structure, and you can always spot them as they move in the direction of the larger trend. To make it easy, we are going to label each wave from this group with numbers from 1 through 5, just like in Image 1.

Since the market is never going to move in just one direction, we are going to see Waves 1, 3, and 5 in the direction of the larger trend and Waves 2 and 4 in the opposite direction. This is going to be the same for all patterns in the Motive Phase group.

For each of the patterns, we only need to learn three rules. The rules are going to be the same for most of them, and we will cover this part shortly.

One thing is certain: after the end of the Motive Pattern, the market is going to start a Corrective Phase. Hence, after we finish this chapter, you are going to know exactly when the trend is going to change.

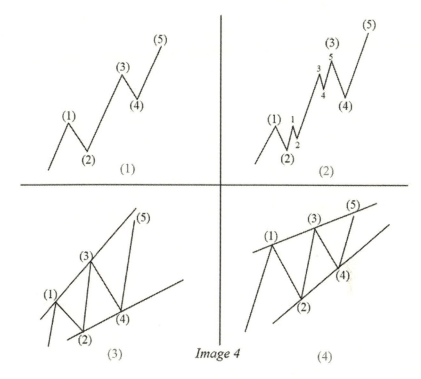

Image 4

In Image 4 above, we have four different patterns: (1) Impulsive Waves, (2) Extended Waves, (3) Leading Diagonals, and (4) Ending Diagonals respectively. We'll separate these patterns into three groups as below.

Impulsive

Impulsive Waves (5-3-5-3-5)

The Impulsive Wave is the first of the four patterns we need to learn and understand. Impulsive Waves have a simple five-wave structure that develops in the direction of the larger trend. Just as with other Motive Patterns, we are going to use numbers from 1 through 5 to label Impulsive Patterns on the chart. After each Impulsive Pattern completes, we are going to see some forms of correction.

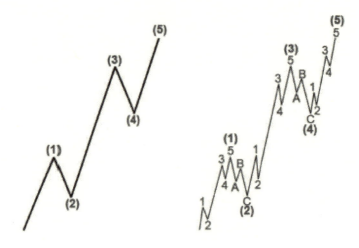

Image 5

From the five-wave structure we have inside of the Impulsive Wave, Waves 1, 3, and 5 are trending moves (in the direction of the larger trend). Waves 2 and 4 are corrective and represent short-term pullbacks in the larger trend.

For each leg of the Impulsive Wave, we will have the exact number of sub-waves you can spot on the smaller timeframes. Inside Waves 1, 3, and 5 we are going to see smaller Motive Patterns (another five-wave structure) and in Waves 2 and 4 we are going to see smaller corrections (another three-wave structure). Look at Image 5 above to get a better understanding of how that would look on a chart.

Now, to be sure that you are labeling Impulsive Waves correctly, you need to remember and cross-check three simple rules.

Impulsive Wave Rules (uptrend)

- **Rule #1** - Wave 2 never falls below the starting point of Wave 1.

- **Rule #2** - Wave 3 is often the longest wave, but never the shortest of the Waves 1-3-5. Wave 3 can be shorter than Wave 1 or Wave 5, but can't be shorter than both.

- **Rule #3** - Wave 4 cannot enter Wave 2 territory.

Impulsive Wave Rules (downtrend)

- **Rule #1** - Wave 2 never goes beyond the starting point of Wave 1.

- **Rule #2** - Wave 3 is often the longest wave, but never the shortest of the Waves 1-3-5. Wave 3 can be shorter than Wave 1 or Wave 5, but can't be shorter than both.

- **Rule #3** - Wave 4 cannot enter Wave 2 territory.

Tip: You can aim at going with Wave 5 after you see some strong and sharp movements (Wave 3 in many cases), but to be sure you are on the right track, make sure all three rules are in place.

Image 6

15

On the daily chart of the AUD/USD pair, we can observe a strong upward movement from 0.8870 to 0.9770. This move has a five-wave structure and appears as an Impulsive Pattern. The main three rules were all respected, and Wave 2 (2w) held above the start of wave 1. Wave 3 (3w) is not the shortest wave (in fact, Wave 3 is the longest wave here) and Wave 4 holds above Wave 2 territory.

Image 7

The main trend on this AUD/USD chart in Image 7 is down, and again we see the five-wave structure from the high at 0.7850 towards 0.7530. Again, we are going to cross-check the rules: Wave 2 holds above the start of Wave 1, Wave 3 is the strongest wave, and Wave 4 holds below the territory of Wave 2.

Now, look at these two examples again and see what the market did after Wave 5 was completed! The market pulled back in what looks like 3 corrective patterns. Until we learn about corrections, I want you just to watch for the 3 corrective patterns against the trend after we complete the Motive Phase.

Extended

Extended Waves (5-3-5-3-5-3-5-3-5)

Usually, one of the Motive Waves (1-3-5) would extend further into another five-wave pattern. At this point, instead of only five waves, we can expect additional moves to have a total nine-wave structure. This type of movement in the market is called Extended Waves.

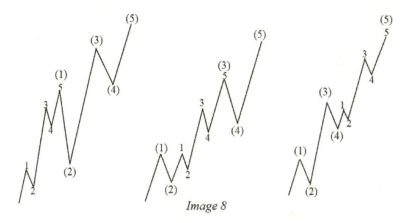

Image 8

Extended Waves appear due to high volatility in the market. You can expect to see extended waves frequently on your charts, especially in the Forex and Stock markets.

Bear in mind that only one wave from Waves 1, 3, and 5 can be extended, so don't try to label two or all three waves as an extension. In many cases, Wave 3 has the best chance to be extended. Every leg of the Extended Waves has the exact number of sub-waves you can spot on the smaller timeframes. Within Waves 1, 3, and 5, we are going to see a smaller Motive Pattern (another five-wave structure) and within Waves 2 and 4, we are going to see smaller corrections (a three-wave structure).

On completion of the nine-wave structure, we would have a complete Motive Pattern, and we can expect a pullback that will take the shape of a correction (three-wave structure).

Extended Wave Rules (uptrend)

- **Rule #1** - Wave 2 never falls below the starting point of Wave 1.
- **Rule #2** - Wave 3 is often the longest wave, but never the shortest of the Waves 1-3, and 5. Wave 3 can be shorter than Wave 1 or Wave 5, but can't be shorter than both.
- **Rule #3** - Wave 4 cannot enter Wave 2 territory.
- **Rule #4** - One of the three impulsive waves is extended.

Extended Wave Rules (downtrend)

- **Rule #1** - Wave 2 never goes beyond the starting point of Wave 1.
- **Rule #2** - Wave 3 is often the longest wave, but never the shortest of the Waves 1-3, and 5. Wave 3 can be shorter than Wave 1 or Wave 5, but can't be shorter than both.
- **Rule #3** - Wave 4 cannot enter Wave 2 territory.
- **Rule #4** - One of the three impulsive waves is extended.

Tip: The strongest volatility in the market occurs after important fundamental events. In many cases, we'll see strong spikes following important news and this is when you can expect to see extended waves.

Image 9

On this daily chart of XAG/USD, we can see a strong upward trend with a Motive pattern. On closer inspection, we can see that we have 9 sub-waves in total, so after checking all the rules, we determine an extended Wave 3 which is labeled from (i) to (v).

Image 10

On this chart of Gold, we have a clean and nice uptrend starting from 1,1184. We will count Wave 1 as the extended wave and is the longest wave of Waves 1, 3, and 5. This, coupled with the fact that Wave 3 is longer than Wave 5, makes the Extended Pattern valid (Wave 3 can be shorter than Wave 1 or Wave 5 but can't be shorter than both Waves 1 and 5).

Diagonals

Leading Diagonals (5-3-5-3-5)

Leading Diagonals (LD) are the first of the two patterns we have in the diagonal group. Just as with each Motive Pattern, LD also has a five-wave structure that moves in the direction of the larger trend. This pattern can only be found in Wave 1 or A (in the case of a Zig-Zag).

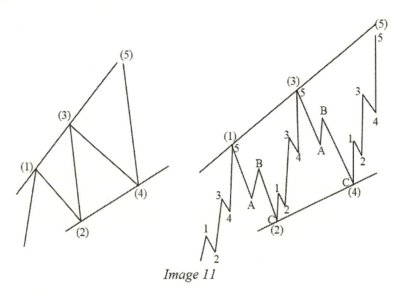

Image 11

What separates Leading Diagonals from Impulsive Waves is Wave 4. In the Leading Diagonals pattern, Wave 4 enters the territory of Wave 2. This occurs because during Wave 1 or A, people are still

20

optimistic about the previous trend and they try to re-enter that market.

The sub-structure is the same as we have in the impulsive pattern. Waves 1, 3, and 5 subdivide further into a smaller five-wave pattern, and Waves 2 and 4 subdivide into smaller corrections. You can refer to the right-hand pattern in Image 11 for an illustration.

Once we've spotted a Leading Diagonal structure, we would have a complete Motive Pattern, and we can expect a pullback that will take the shape of a correction (three-wave structure). After a Leading Diagonal, there is usually a deeper pullback expected.

Leading Diagonal Rules (uptrend)

- **Rule #1** - Wave 2 never falls below the starting point of Wave 1.

- **Rule #2** - Wave 3 is often the longest, but never the shortest of the Waves 1-3-5. Wave 3 can be shorter than Wave 1 or Wave 5, but can't be shorter than both.

- **Rule #3** - Wave 4 must hold above the end of Wave 2.

Leading Diagonal Rules (downtrend)

- **Rule #1** - Wave 2 never goes beyond the starting point of Wave 1.

- **Rule #2** - Wave 3 is often the longest, but never the shortest of the Waves 1-3-5. Wave 3 can be shorter than Wave 1 or Wave 5, but can't be shorter than both.

- **Rule #3** - Wave 4 must hold below the end of Wave 2.

Tip: Since we know that LD patterns appear only inside of Wave 1 or A, and we know that Wave 1 starts when the trend is changing, we can expect to see this type of move in the opposite direction of the trend or when the trend ends.

Image 12

In the example above, we have a five-wave move to the downside. Notice Wave 1 has five sub-waves in it, and Wave 4 has entered the territory of Wave 2 (breaks above the horizontal line), so we can't categorize this move into an Impulsive or Extended wave. Since Wave 1 can be determined as a larger one, we can refer to the pattern as a Leading Diagonal pattern.

But again, don't forget that Wave 2 needs to remain below the start of Wave 1, Wave 3 can't be the shortest one, and Wave 4 must end below the ending point of Wave 2. We understand that after a five-wave downward move, we should expect three upward waves. However, as long as the price holds below the start of Wave 1, we can continue to watch for more bearish movements.

Ending Diagonal (3-3-3-3-3)

This pattern occurs during the Motive Phase and they also form part of the diagonal group. Just as we had a Leading Diagonal at the start of the trend, the Ending Diagonal is the pattern that appears in the ending stages of the trend, in either Wave 5 or Wave C.

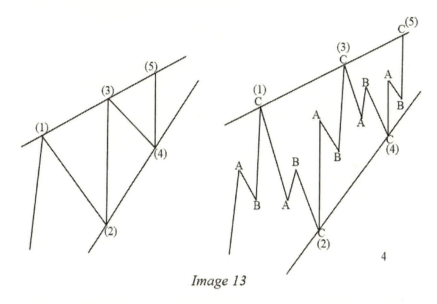

Image 13

Similar to the LDs, we have a five-wave structure that moves in a direction of the market, and Wave 4 needs to test the territory of Wave 2. The biggest difference between the Ending Diagonal and the rest of the Motive Patterns is the number of required sub-waves.

Inside each leg of the Ending Diagonal (Waves 1, 2, 3, 4, and 5), we have a smaller number of sub-waves (a three-wave structure).

Once we've spotted a Leading Diagonal structure, we would complete finding the Motive Pattern, so we can expect a pullback that will take the form of a correction (a three-wave structure).

Ending Diagonal Rules (uptrend)

- **Rule #1** - Wave 2 never falls below the starting point of Wave 1.

23

- **Rule #2** - Wave 3 is often the longest, but never the shortest of the Waves 1-3-5. Wave 3 can be shorter than Wave 1 or Wave 5, but can't be shorter than both.

- **Rule #3** - Wave 4 can enter the Wave 2 territory but must hold above the end of Wave 2.

Ending Diagonal Rules (downtrend)

- **Rule #1** - Wave 2 never goes beyond the starting point of Wave 1.

- **Rule #2** - Wave 3 is often the longest, but never the shortest of the Waves 1-3-5. Wave 3 can be shorter than Wave 1 or Wave 5, but can't be shorter than both.

- **Rule #3** - Wave 4 can enter the Wave 2 territory but must hold below the end of Wave 2.

Tip: *The easiest way to spot the Ending Diagonal on a blank chart would be to look out for a Wedge Pattern. Wedge Patterns appear at the ending stages of the trend, and usually, that's where you can spot five waves with 3 sub-waves within!*

EUR/USD
1-hour chart

Image 14

On the EUR/USD chart above, we can observe strong and sharp bullish movements before a trend reversal appeared at the right of the chart. Right before the drop, there was a contest going on between buyers and sellers. Looking at the number of waves we have from the end of Wave 4, we'll see a five-wave structure [labeled (i) to (v)].

On the chart, you can clearly see that Wave (iii) is longer than Wave (i), meaning that rule 2 has been complied with. Moreover, since the price movements in Wave (iv) drop to test the territory of Wave (ii), we identify this as an Ending Diagonal.

After the breakout of the lower trend line of the Wedge Pattern, we spot a solid three-wave move.

So, we've gone through five types of Motive Phases in the Elliott Wave cycle. Honestly, identifying different types of Motive Phases is not a challenging task, but it needs practicing again and again. You should go over each of them and try to spot them on as many charts as possible before you move on to cover the second phase of the Elliott Wave Theory: **The Corrective Phase.**

Now you may understand how to identify some patterns of the Motive Phase. However, the markets don't just move in the same direction all the time, hence we need to take a look at the second phase: the Corrective Phase.

An easy way to remember the Corrective Phase would be to think of these patterns as a three-wave move against the primary trend.

To visually separate the Corrective Phase from the Motive Phase on the charts, let's label these patterns using the letters A, B, and C. Of the three waves, Waves A and C will move in the same direction, and that's usually going to be against the larger trend, and Wave B will be the correction in the middle.

There are a few more patterns to be learned in this phase, and we'll discover their rules and the best way to find them.

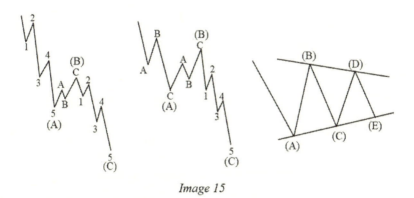

Image 15

Again, we are going to separate all the patterns into smaller groups so that they are easier to learn and understand. An easy way to name these patterns would be as Simple Corrections (Zig-Zag, Flat, and Triangle) and Complex Corrections (Double & Triple Three).

The main difference with the Corrective Patterns would be the number of sub-waves in waves A-B-C. For every pattern, you'll have an exact number of sub-waves you need to find, and I strongly suggest you try to memorize them as soon as possible.

1. Simple Correction

Zig-Zag Correction (5-3-5)

What is a Zig-Zag correction?

The Zig-Zag (ZZ) correction is the first pattern of the Corrective Phase you need to learn. Generally, this is the easiest type of correction to learn since it has a lot in common with Motive Waves. Zig-Zag corrections have a simple three-wave structure labeled as A -B-C.

Waves A and C are both Motive in nature and have five sub-waves within. Usually, they form an Impulsive Wave. Wave B is another correction, and within that three-smaller waves, either another small Zig-Zag or Triangle can be formed.

You will notice that Zig-Zags have the same number of sub-waves as the 1-2-3 pattern, however, what separates the A-B-C from the 1-2-3 pattern is the end of Wave C. Within a Zig-Zag, C is usually going to be equal in size to Wave A, while in a Motive Phase, Wave 3 is usually the longest.

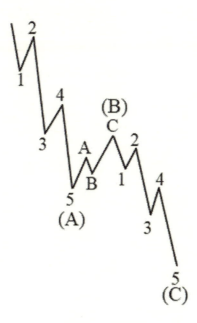

Image 16

A Zig-Zag correction is a common pattern to find in Waves 2, 4, and B.

Zig-Zag Correction Rules (correction in an uptrend)

- **Rule #1** - Wave B must end below the start of Wave A.
- **Rule #2** - Wave C must break below the end of Wave A.

Zig-Zag Correction Rules (correction in a downtrend)

- **Rule #1** - Wave B must end above the start of Wave A.
- **Rule #2** - Wave C must break above the end of Wave A.

Image 17

On the USD/JPY example above, we can see a three-wave correction to the upside, and the first and third legs are more or less equal. There isn't a big difference between them, and that's the main reason why we decide on it being a Zig-Zag. Now we have five waves in A, three waves in B, and five waves in C. After this correction, we expect to see an Impulsive Wave move downwards.

Image 18

This USD/MXN example in Image 18 is one of the clearest on how to find the ZZ. After a top that occurred around August 25th, this exotic pair developed its first five-wave structure lower, and if you didn't understand the larger count, you might say that we are ending either Wave 1 or Wave A, right? Next, we have a consolidation that looks like a Triangle, and since we know that Wave 2 can't be a Triangle... it follows then that a Zig-Zag in Wave B is the only option! Finally, we see a five-wave move within Wave C. It is virtually equal to those of Wave A.

Flat Correction (3-3-5)

What is a Flat correction?

The Flat correction is also one of the simpler Corrective Patterns. In this pattern, we can categorize into three different three-wave structures as labeled in the picture below.

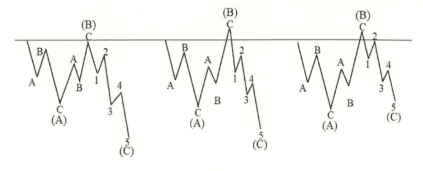

Image 19

Waves A and B in the Flat correction are both corrective in nature, so we need to see three waves inside each of these legs. In about 90% of cases, both Waves A and B are just going to be smaller Zig-Zag corrections, but you can also expect other types of corrections inside these such as Flat or Complex corrections. Wave C is the only Motive Pattern, so we can expect five waves in the final leg.

Flat Correction Rules

Flat corrections have a few different variations but they all have one thing in common: Wave B in the Flat needs to test at least 90% of Wave A if we are to call the pattern valid (you can allow 78.6% as the minimum in the Forex market).

We have three patterns in the Flat group: Regular, Expanding & Running. Although they are all very similar, there is a slight change between them.

What is a Regular Flat Correction?

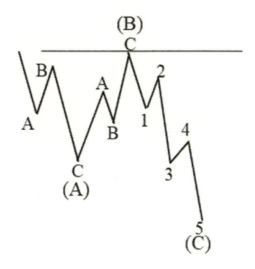

Image 20

Regular Flats have three waves against the larger trend. They have three waves in A, three waves in B, and five waves in C. For the Regular Flat to be valid, Wave B needs to end at least at 90% of Wave A (78.6% is allowed in the Forex market), but should not exceed the start of Wave A.

Regular FLAT Rules (correction in an uptrend)

- **Rule #1** - Wave B must retrace to 90% of Wave A (78.6% allowed in Forex).

- **Rule #2** - Wave C must end below the end of Wave A.

Regular FLAT Rules (correction in a downtrend)

- **Rule #1** - Wave B must retrace to 90% of Wave A (78.6% allowed in Forex).

- **Rule #2** - Wave C must end above the end of Wave A.

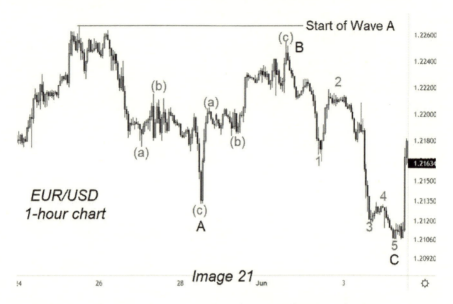

Image 21

In the image above, we can see that the EUR/USD pair made a three-wave move from 1.2270 to 1.2135 (Wave A). We have a deep pullback in Wave B (also a three-wave move) before a large Wave C occurred. Notice how Wave C includes five sub-waves that broke below the end of Wave A. All of these bring about a regular flat in this case.

Expanding Flat Correction

What is an Expanding Flat correction?

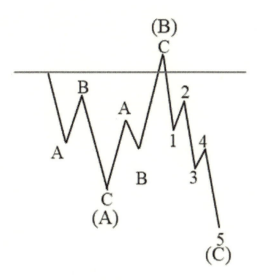

Image 22

The Expanding Flat patterns have the same number of sub-waves as a Regular Flat: three waves in A, three waves in B, and five waves in C. The only difference is with the end of Wave B. In this type of correction, Wave B often exceeds the start of Wave A (ideally between the inverse of 123.6% and 161.8% of Wave A).

Expanding Flat Pattern Rules (correction in an uptrend)

- **Rule #1** - Wave B needs to break through the starting level of Wave A, but can't end above an inverse of 161.8% of Wave A.

- **Rule #2** - Wave C needs to end below the ending level of Wave A.

Expanding Flat Pattern Rules (correction in a downtrend)

- **Rule #1** - Wave B needs to break through the starting level of Wave A, but can't end below an inverse of 161.8% of Wave A.

- **Rule #2** - Wave C needs to end above the ending level of Wave A.

Image 23

Take the daily AUD/USD chart above as an example. We have an ascending three-wave move in Wave A and a breakout below the start of Wave A, but movements still look bullish, so I labeled that next three-wave move as Wave B. Lastly, we have a five-wave upward move in Wave C. Because the price action in Wave B was corrective in nature and broke through the starting level of Wave A, we categorize this as an Expanding Flat.

36

Running Flat Correction

What is a Running Flat correction?

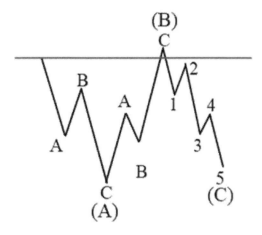

Image 24

The Running Flat is the same as the Expanding Flat in structure. We have three waves in Wave A, three waves in Wave B that end above the starting level of Wave A, and five waves within Wave C. The difference between them is only found with the ending of Wave C. In the Running Flat pattern, Wave C cannot exceed the ending level of Wave A.

Running Flat Pattern Rules (correction in an uptrend)

- **Rule #1** - Wave B needs to go beyond the starting level of Wave A, but cannot end above an inverse of 161.8% of Wave A.

- **Rule #2** - Wave C needs to hold above the ending level of Wave A.

Running Flat Pattern Rules (correction in a downtrend)

- **Rule #1** - Wave B needs to fall below the starting level of Wave A, but cannot end below an inverse of 161.8% of Wave A.

- **Rule #2** - Wave C needs to hold below the ending level of Wave A.

Of the three flat patterns, I want you to focus on the Regular and Expanding Flats. Running Flats are really rare patterns to see, especially with the current high volatility in all the markets. You would label a pattern as a Running Flat only if you can't determine any other correction.

Image 25

On the chart above, you can see that Wave B broke above the starting point of Wave A. Moreover, although Wave C includes some strong bearish candlesticks, it failed to break below the end of Wave A. All of these conditions together contribute to the formation of a Running Flat pattern on the EUR/USD daily chart.

Triangle Correction (3-3-3-3-3)

The Triangle correction is the final type of the Simple Correction group that we are going to cover. Up until now, we've only learned about corrections that have three-wave structures. With triangles, we need to add two more waves, so every triangle will need to have a five-wave structure. We are also going to use the letters A-B-C-D-E to label this type of movement on the charts.

Triangles are patterns that appear usually in the middle and at the ending stages of the trend, and they can only be seen in Wave 4 in a Motive Phase and Waves B & X (will be learned shortly) in a Corrective Phase.

There are four different types of triangle patterns we need to learn. To better understand every triangle pattern, let's take a look at the image below.

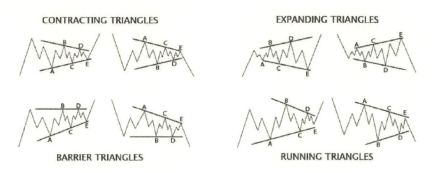

Image 26

When examining each of these triangles we'll notice some differences.

Contracting Triangles

What is a Contracting Triangle?

Contracting triangles are the simplest five-wave triangle, where each of the triangle's legs is smaller than the previous one (A is the biggest).

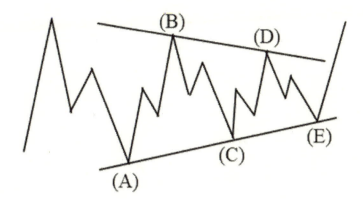

Image 27

Contracting Triangle Rules

- **Rule #1** - Wave B must be smaller than Wave A

- **Rule #2** - Wave C must be smaller than Wave B

- **Rule #3** - Wave D must be smaller than Wave C

- **Rule #4** - Wave E must be smaller than Wave D

<u>Barrier Triangles</u>

What is a Barrier Triangle?

A Barrier triangle is similar to a Contracting triangle. This is also a five-wave triangle. The main difference is Wave B and Wave D need to end at similar levels. When you draw a trend line connecting B and D, you'll have a strong (horizontal) resistance level.

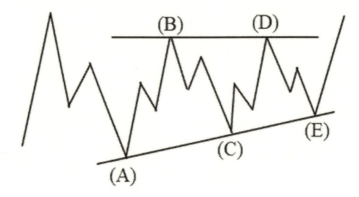

Image 28

Barrier Triangle Rules

- **Rule #1** - Wave B must be smaller than Wave A

- **Rule #2** - Wave C must be smaller than Wave B

- **Rule #3** - Wave D must be smaller than Wave C

- **Rule #4** - Wave E must be smaller than Wave D

- **Rule #5** – Wave B and Wave D are located at similar levels.

<u>*Running Triangles*</u>

What is a Running Triangle?

Running triangles are the same as Contracting Triangles with one small difference. Wave B ends slightly above the starting level of Wave A. In many cases, it's the result of a short-term spike in the market caused by a fundamental event.

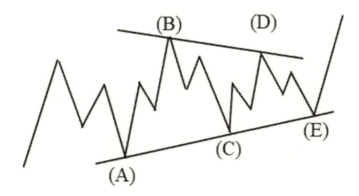

Image 29

Running Triangle Rules (correction in an uptrend)

- **Rule #1** - Wave B must end above the start of Wave A.
- **Rule #2** - Wave C must be smaller than Wave B.
- **Rule #3** - Wave D must be smaller than Wave C.
- **Rule #4** - Wave E must be smaller than Wave D.

Running Triangle Rules (correction in a downtrend)

- **Rule #1** - Wave B must end below the start of Wave A.
- **Rule #2** - Wave C must be smaller than Wave B.
- **Rule #3** - Wave D must be smaller than Wave C.
- **Rule #4** - Wave E must be smaller than Wave D.

What is an Expanding Triangle?

Expanding triangles are five-wave triangles in which each leg of the triangle is larger than the previous one (A is the smallest). Just think of this triangle as the mirror of a Contracting triangle.

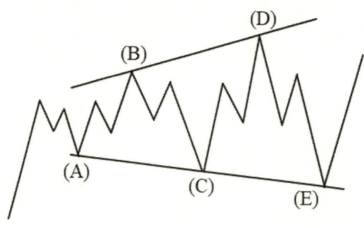

Image 30

Expanding Triangle Rules

- **Rule #1** - Wave B must be larger than Wave A.

- **Rule #2** - Wave C must be larger than Wave B.

- **Rule #3** - Wave D must be larger than Wave C.

- **Rule #4** - Wave E must be larger than Wave D.

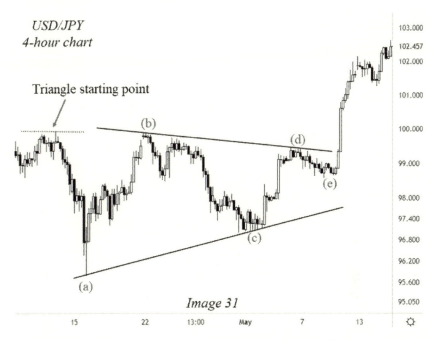

USD/JPY
4-hour chart

Triangle starting point

(b)

(d)

(e)

(c)

(a)

Image 31

The USD/JPY pair is famous for triangles, and here's an example of just one of the triangles found. We can see that there are five waves in total and that each leg is smaller than the previous one. Therefore, we can call this pattern a Contracting Triangle!

Image 32

This triangle on the price of Gold looks similar to the triangle on the previous example. However, when looking closer at the ending point of Wave B, you can see that it ends above the starting point of Wave A. I would therefore label this as a Running Triangle.

Also, on both previous charts, note the reactions of price when breaking through the triangles. In both pairs, we see a strong and sharp movement in the direction of the larger trend.

2. Complex Correction

Now, let's move on to a more complicated section of the Corrective Phase: Complex Corrections. This is more complex as there are many options, but unfortunately, not as many rules were explained by R.N. Elliott. I attempted to make this section as simple as possible so that you don't need to spend too much time on it.

Within Complex Corrections, we have two patterns: Double Three and Triple Three Corrections.

The Double Three correction develops when there's a three-wave pattern where each wave has three smaller sub-waves.

The Triple Three correction develops from five waves, where again each leg has three smaller sub-waves.

To separate Complex Corrections from simple Corrective Patterns we are going to use the following labels: W-X-Y for the Double pattern and W-X-Y-X-Z for the Triple pattern.

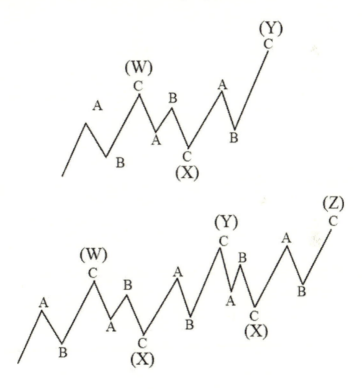

Image 33

Until you're sure that you can recognize the simple Corrective Patterns well, I don't want you to even bother with these sorts of corrections. Ideally, I prefer that you not concern yourself with them for the first couple of weeks from when you learned about Elliott Wave.

Below are all that I believe you'll need to understand about each of these two Corrective Patterns.

Double Three (3-3-3)

What is a Double Three?

A Double Three correction is made up of three-wave moves, like the Zig-Zag or Flat, however, each leg (W, X, and Y) will be a different correction. The easiest way to imagine it is to ask yourself how this pattern would fit on a chart showing market movement. Imagine a correction, after correction, after correction.

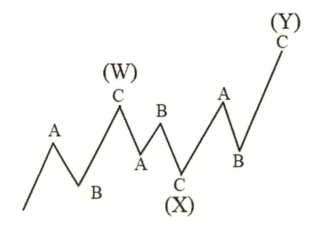

Image 34

This type of correction is commonly spotted in Wave 4 if Wave 2 is a simple correction such as a Zig-Zag or Flat.

Patterns to Expect In Each Leg:

- Wave W can be either a Zig-Zag or Flat correction

- Wave X can be either a Zig-Zag, Flat, or Triangle correction

- Wave Y can be either a Zig-Zag, Flat, or Triangle.

Each of the waves could become another complex correction, but if you start analyzing each wave in this manner, you can get confused as to where the market is really headed with many options. Hence, I strongly suggest that you never try to force yourself to determine Complex Corrections within other Complex Corrections.

We don't have many rules from Mr. Elliott concerning Complex Corrections. However, I have some rules that I use in order to make the determination of complex corrections less subjective. Here are the main rules that I think you need to follow.

Double Three Rules (correction in a downtrend)

- **Rule #1** - Wave X must end above the starting level of Wave W.

- **Rule #2** - Wave Y must end above the ending level of Wave W.

Double Three Rules (correction in an uptrend)

- **Rule #1** - Wave X must end below the starting level of Wave W.

- **Rule #2** - Wave Y must end below the ending level of Wave W.

Image 35

On the EUR/USD chart above, the movements appear really sharp, and you might ask yourself why I would be labeling this as a Double Three pattern. Within Wave (W), we have a Zig-Zag (5-3-5) pattern, then we have 3 downward waves in Wave (X), and another Zig-Zag within Wave (Y). The movements look impulsive, however, the larger picture is still corrective and once Wave (Y) ended, the EUR/USD pair started to decline.

50

Triple Three (3-3-3-3-3)

What is a Triple Three?

The Triple Three correction is the final pattern of the Corrective Phase in this chapter.

Triple Three corrections have a five-wave structure that moves against the direction of the larger trend.

The easiest way to learn and understand this pattern would be to associate it with the Ending Diagonal. They both have the same number of sub-waves, and the only difference between them is where you would see them on a chart. The Ending Diagonal develops in the direction of the larger trend while the Triple Three is against the trend.

This type of correction is commonly detected in Wave 4 if Wave 2 was a simple correction such as a Zig-Zag or Flat.

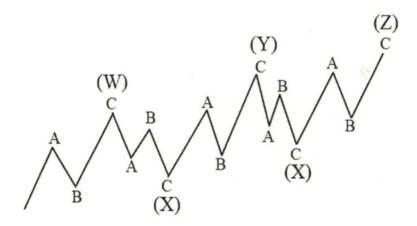

Image 36

Patterns to Expect In Each Leg:

- Wave W can be either a Zig-Zag or Flat correction.

- Wave X can be either a Zig-Zag, Flat, or Triangle correction.

- Wave Y can be either a Zig-Zag or Flat correction.

- Wave X2 can be either a Zig-Zag, Flat, or Triangle.

- Wave Z can be either a Zig-Zag, Flat, or Triangle

Again, each of the waves could become another complex correction if you start analyzing each wave. However, doing this, one can get confused as to where the market is heading with many options. So, I strongly suggest that you never try to force yourself to determine Complex Corrections within other Complex Corrections.

Triple Three Rules (correction in a downtrend)

- **Rule #1** - Wave X must end above the starting level of Wave W.

- **Rule #2** - Wave Y must end above the ending level of Wave W.

- **Rule #3** - Wave X2 must end above the starting level of Wave Y.

- **Rule #4** - Wave Z must end above the starting level of Wave Y.

Triple Three Rules (correction in an uptrend)

- **Rule #1** - Wave X must end below the starting level of Wave W.

- **Rule #2** - Wave Y must end below the ending level of Wave W.

- **Rule #3** - Wave X2 must end below the starting level of Wave Y.

- **Rule #4** - Wave Z must end below the starting level of Wave Y.

Image 37

We might rarely see the Triple three pattern on a chart. However, to demonstrate it, observe my alternate count for GOLD in the image above. Over a few years, almost everyone seemed to give up on this commodity and almost every move looked corrective in nature. When you count how many three-wave movements are connected, you will see that the count is 5 (W-X-Y-X-Z), and the only thing you can label it would be some sort of complex correction.

A Simple Trick In Identifying Complex Corrections!

I want to make your life as easy as I possibly can, and there is a "trick" to assist in the determination of a Double Three correction without really needing to verify if Wave W is a Zig-Zag or if Wave X is one of the other patterns.

Take another look at the image of the Double Three correction below and start counting the waves as you would count your higher highs and lower lows…

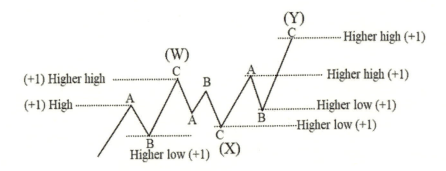

Image 38

If we start at Wave (W) we can count Wave A as High (+1), Wave B as Higher Low (+1), and Wave C as Higher High (+1). Next, we have Wave (X) which has 3 smaller waves, and C is the Higher Low compared to B in Wave (W) so that's another +1. And, in the final Wave (Y), again we have Wave A as a Higher High, which gives us (+1). Wave B is the Higher Low (+1) and Wave C is another Higher High (+1). Now, we have **seven waves** (7 times +1) in total!

To sum up, to identify a complex correction more easily, you'll want to wait until you have **seven waves** against the trend. You will then understand that this is Double Three, and can start to buy/sell in the direction of the larger trend.

Image 39

In the chart image above, the EUR/USD has been trading in a strong downward trend, so corrections should be seen as higher pushes. Now, if you were to check the Higher Highs and Higher Lows, you would see that from levels 1.0780 to 1.0985, we have seven waves, but let's break that down again step-by-step.

Leg 1 is the first high we see (+1), after that Wave 2 is a Higher Low (+1).

The third leg represents a Higher High (+1) and leg 4 represents a Higher Low (+1).

Wave 5 is a Higher High (+1) while Wave 6 represents a Higher Low (+1). Finally, Wave 7 represents a Higher High (+1).

In total: we have seven waves: High + Higher Low + Higher High + Higher Low + Higher High + Higher Low + Higher High. You know then that you have Wave W at the end of Wave 3, Wave X at end of Wave 4, and Wave Y at the end of Wave 7.

So, we've completed all the patterns in the Corrective Phase in the Elliott Wave Cycle. It seems more complicated than the Motive Phase, but don't worry, you'll master it after a lot of practice with different charts. One important thing to note is not all patterns share

55

the same popularity. There are some which are more commonly spotted on the chart, while others rarely appear. Anyway, this chapter has brought everything you'll need to know about the Corrective Phase, and you can now categorize nearly every price fluctuation on the chart into different corrective patterns.

CHAPTER IV: ELLIOTT WAVE OPTIMIZATION

Elliott Wave Theory is important in helping you to anticipate in what direction the market will move. Using Elliott Wave, you would be able to know how many waves the trend has been experiencing and whether we should expect a Motive Phase or Corrective Phase within the next price fluctuations.

Yet, trend determination is not enough in trading.

One of the most challenging tasks in technical analysis is identifying entry and exit points. We need to determine around which price level there might be a higher potential of a price reaction, or a trend reversal to enter and exit trades. In this respect, there is more than one tool to combine with Elliott Wave to produce the best results. This chapter will discuss how combining Elliott Wave with some powerful technical tools and chart patterns can facilitate wave count and the determination of potential trade setups, as well as provide more options in trading with the trend.

1. Fibonacci Tools

Among the most popular Fibonacci tools in trading are Fibonacci retracements and extensions. The Fibonacci tools are named after the famous Italian mathematician Leonardo Pisano Bogollo, who was widely known as Leonardo Fibonacci. The magical sequence for calculating Fibonacci ratios in trading goes like this:

0, 1, 1, 2, 3, 5, 8, 13, 21, 34, 55, 89, 144, 233, 377, 610, 987... with the string continuing indefinitely.

It should be noted that Fibonacci didn't create this sequence. Instead, he introduced the string to Western Europe in the 13th century after learning about them from the Indian merchants. It is believed that the Fibonacci sequence was first formulated between 450 and 200 BCE.

The Fibonacci levels are mainly derived from the number string above (except for the 50% level). With an exception of the first few numbers, diving a number by the next one yields approximately 0.618, or 61.8%. When we divide a number by the second number to its right, the result is around 0.382 or 38.2%. Dividing a number by the third number to its right yields approximately 0.236, or 23.6%. By learning about the relationship between the numbers in the sequence, we get some golden ratios that assist us in defining the retracement or extension degree of the price.

Fibonacci Numbers You Should Be Aware Of

The most commonly used Fibonacci levels that we're going to use with Elliott Wave are:

23.6%; 38.2%; 50.0%; 61.8%; 78.6%; 100.0%; 123.6%; 161.8%; 200%.

Fibonacci (Fib) Tools & Elliott Wave

You only need two tools to find the potential ends of waves:

- **Fibonacci Retracement**
- **Fibonacci Extensions**

The Fibonacci Retracement Tool

The Fibonacci Retracement Tool will assist us to determine the potential ending points of the corrective Waves: 2-4-B-X. The best use of this tool lies in finding potential entry points for the next wave and making sure that we'll trade in the direction of the larger trend.

Using this tool is simple across all platforms. You draw Fibs from the start to the end of the previous trend wave (the price swing). For example, if you want to find the end of Wave 2, you'll draw Fibs from the start to the end of Wave 1.

Image 40

Fibonacci Expansion Tool

The Fibonacci Expansion Tool will assist us to determine potential ending points of the Waves: 3-5-C. The best use of this tool lies in locating potential exits points for your trades.

Using this tool is simple across all platforms. You draw Fibs from the start to the end of the previous trend wave/ swing and then project from a pullback. For example: If you want to find the end of Wave 3, you'll draw Fibs from the start to the end of Wave 1 and project from the end of Wave 2.

Image 41

Note: At the end of the book, there is a detailed appendix about how to draw Fibonacci retracement and expansion levels.

Motive Wave Fibonacci Levels to Watch

- **Wave 2 Fibonacci Levels:** Wave 2 often ends between 50% and 61.8% of Wave 1 (minimum 38.2%).

- **Wave 3 Fibonacci Levels:** Wave 3 often ends between 161.8% and 200% of Wave 1 (minimum 100%).

- **Wave 4 Fibonacci Levels:** Wave 4 often ends between 23.6% and 38.2% of Wave 3.

- **Wave 5 Fibonacci Levels:** Wave 5 often ends between inverse 100% and 161.8% of Wave 4.

Corrective Wave Fibonacci Levels to Watch

- **Zig-Zag Correction Levels:** Wave B often ends between 50% - 61.8% of Wave A. Wave C often ends between 100%-123.6% of Wave A.

- **Flat Correction Levels:** Wave B often ends between 78.6% and 90% of Wave A in a Regular correction and between inverse 123.6% and 161.8% of Wave A in an Expanding & Running correction.

  Wave C often ends between 100% and 123.6% of Wave A in a Regular correction, and 161.8% of the B target in an Expanding correction.

- **Triangle Correction Levels:** Wave C often ends at 61.8% of Wave A. Wave D often ends at 61.8% of Wave B. Wave E often ends at 61.8% of Wave C.

- **Complex Correction Levels:** Wave X often ends between 50% - 61.8% of Wave W. Wave Y often ends between 100% - 123.6% of Wave W. Wave X2 often ends between 50% - 61.8% of Wave Y. Wave Z often ends between 100% - 123.6% of Wave Y.

We'll go deeper into how to use these retracement levels in the next chapter. In the next section, let's discover some other effective chart patterns and tools to combine with Elliott Wave.

2. Elliott Wave Trading With Chart Patterns And Technical Tools

We can now anticipate in which direction the market is going to move. We know potential targets, where to expect the ends of pullbacks and trends and now you've got to be asking yourself this question: "It's all great, but how and where do I start looking for all these patterns?"

There are actually many ways that you can start searching for potential setups in the financial markets. I've tried some methods, but I find that only one method has really worked so far.

Here are the main three steps you need to find your major setups.

- **Step #1** - Use the High Low Method;

- **Step #2** - Watch for Simple Patterns;

- **Step #3** - Validate Counts with Indicators.

Let's now go through these step-by-step!

Method #1 - Using the High Low Method

Until now, you've probably grasped the most important task: You can expect to see the Motive Phase in the direction of the larger trend and the Corrective Phase in the opposite direction of the larger trend. So, your first task is going to be to learn how to identify the start of the trend.

The best way to do this is by opening a plain chart for any instrument you plan to label and finding significant turning points. The next two charts are great examples of valid turning points.

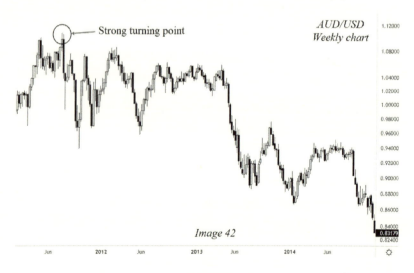

Image 42

The chart above shows the best turning point that you can pick for finding the start of an Elliott wave count on the AUD/USD chart. As you can see, we've found the beginning of the descending trend at the start of a long bearish candlestick.

Image 43

In this example, the EUR/CHF pair started this upward trend a few days after the Swiss National Bank crash, so you could pick this level as the starting point of your wave count.

Now that you've defined your starting point, look at the chart from that point up until the current market price and ask yourself this simple question: "Does this move look to be Motive or Corrective?"

Image 44

If you see sharp, strong movements, you can conclude **Motive**. In case you see choppy, overlapping movements, you can conclude: **Corrective**. Try not to spend hours on this step with each trade. The maximum time I would spend would be 10-15 seconds. If you are not sure of the answer, just move on to the next chart.

If you concluded Motive, try to find one of the four types of Motive Patterns on the chart. Just label them 1-2-3-4-5 and start cross-checking the rules. If you concluded Corrective, determine what pattern from the Corrective groups would best fit on your chart.

You might not always be correct, however. That's why you have these rules to assist, and only when ALL rules match can you then enter into a trade.

Method #2 Patterns & Elliott Waves

The Elliott Wave strategy is nothing more than a pattern-trading game. Traders, however, tend to make everything more complicated than it should be. There are many simple patterns that you should be aware of such as Head & Shoulders, Double Tops, Triangle & Wedge Patterns. If you know how to find them on your charts, you won't have any trouble learning to identify wave patterns within just a few minutes.

Head and Shoulders (H&S) & Wave Map

Head and Shoulders is the pattern that I believe every trader knows. If you spot them, go and check what type of wave it represents.

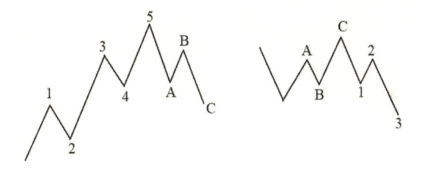

Image 45

- **First Probability** - H&S represents the end of a Motive wave and a Correction.

- **Second Probability** - H&S represents the end of a Correction and the start of an Impulsive Wave.

Tip: Check how many waves you can see from the nearest turning point. If you see five waves from the bottom towards the head, you can make the first conclusion. If you see just three waves from the bottom towards the head, you can make the second conclusion.

Image 46

In this example, from the closest bottom towards the H&S head, there are five waves, hence we choose the first probability.

Double Top & Wave Map

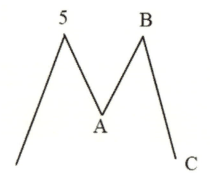

Image 47

Double Tops have two tops that end around a similar level. Moreover, since the right top doesn't end above the left top, this would best fit the description of the FLAT correction.

Option – The left top represents Wave 5, the pullback in the middle: Wave A, the right top: Wave B, the final drop: Wave C.

Tip: Cross-check how many waves you can see from the nearest turning point. If you see five waves from the bottom towards the head, you could conclude this is a Flat.

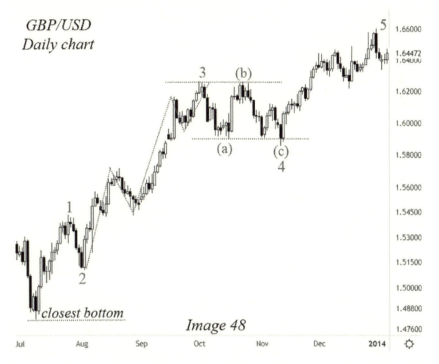

Image 48

Sometimes, we don't find exactly five waves. However, within Wave 3, we have 5 smaller waves, so we can fit the FLAT correction inside Wave 4 as depicted in the image above.

We've already discussed the fact that wedges best match up with an Ending Diagonal. Moreover, since Ending Diagonals either occur in Wave 5 or Wave C, these are the two options we are going to use.

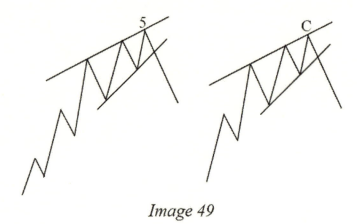

Image 49

- **First Probability** –The Wedge represents the end of Wave 5.

- **Second Probability** – The Wedge represents the end of Wave C.

Tip: Check how many waves you can see from the nearest turning point. If you see five waves from the bottom towards the head then it should be the first probability. If you can see just three waves from the bottom towards the head, it should be the second probability.

Image 50

In the image above, from the nearest bottom toward the end of the Wedge Pattern, there are five waves, and the Ending Diagonal forms part of Wave 5.

Triangle & Wave Maps

Triangles appear only in Waves 4 & B.

- **First Probability** – The Triangle represents the end of Wave 4.

- **Second Probability** – The Triangle represents the end of Wave B.

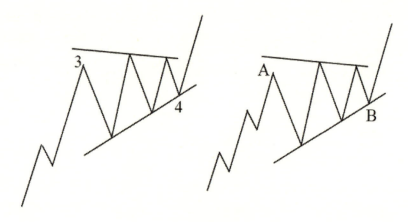

Image 51

Tip: *Check how many waves you can see from the nearest turning point. If you see three waves from the bottom toward the start of the triangle, it should be the first probability. If you see the complete five waves from the bottom toward the start of the Triangle, it should be the second probability.*

Image 52

We see a Triangle pattern developing in this crude oil chart in Image 52. Before the triangle appears, we have five waves already completed, so we can opt for the second probability and try to determine whether this would be an A-B-C Zig-Zag correction.

Method #3 Indicators & Elliott Waves

Indicators are some of the most commonly used tools among technical analysts. An indicator can be simply defined as a mathematical calculation based on the price movement or volume of the asset or instrument. With technical indicators, you are trying to predict future price movements based on past price fluctuations. Among the most commonly used indicators are Moving Average (MA), Relative Strength Index (RSI), MACD, and Stochastic Oscillator. However, as I tend to keep the chart as clean as possible, we are going to use the RSI indicator to assist us in validating our wave counts.

Relative Strength Index

The Relative Strength Index, or RSI for short, is one of the basic indicators that most traders use every day. This oscillator identifies oversold and overbought areas and, like many oscillators, the RSI scales from 0 to 100. If the reading moves below 30, we say that the market is "oversold", and if the indicator moves above 70, we say it is "overbought". However, in my strategy, I don't want you to focus too much on these levels. The thing I really want you to learn is *how to spot divergence with RSI.*

Image 53

On the Oil chart above, we can see that the price action developed a higher High while the RSI indicated a lower High during the same period. This is a typical example of divergence in a bullish trend.

Gold
Daily chart

380.00
372.00
364.00
356.00
348.50
346.00
342.50
336.50
330.50
324.50
319.00

Low

Lower low

80.00
60.00
40.00

Higher low

Low

Image 54

Apr   Jun

On the Gold chart above, the price action of Gold developed one lower Low, but the RSI oscillator releases a higher reading during the same period, forming a typical example of divergence in a bearish trend.

To use the RSI indicator in validating your wave counts, simply look for divergence. We know that Wave 3 is often the strongest wave among all, and the momentum may fall between Wave 3 and 5. Therefore, the zone between these two waves is a potential area for divergence to appear. In the event of an extended wave pattern, the RSI may start to show divergence from the Wave 3 of Wave 3 through the end of Wave 5.

73

Image 55

On the EUR/USD chart above, there are some upwards movements that I've labeled as extended waves. According to the rules, we need to see divergence from the end of Wave (iii) (of 3) to the end of Wave 5. Such divergence is spotted very easily, and we may see a pullback very soon after the divergence appears.

Image 56

The GBP/JPY chart above shows an Impulsive Wave. However, to be sure that we are right, we need to see divergence between Wave 3 and Wave 5. In this case, we have divergence even before Wave 3 ended (ideally be from the end of the smaller (iii) of 3). All we actually need to concern ourselves with is that divergence gives you an additional layer of confirmation that you are on the right track.

Combining All Together!

Of the three methods, there is not really any that could be regarded as the "best".

Your best option might be to combine all three methods at the same time. It's always great to have as much confirmation as you can before you enter a trade. Let's now see how that would work in a live market condition below.

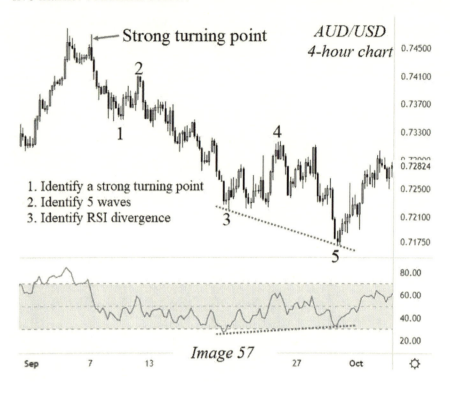

Image 57

One of the most difficult parts of any trading course or book is delivering the right strategy to the right trader. A scalper won't apply the swing trading strategies effectively, and a long-term trader never prefers a day trading strategy. In trading, there are two noticeable trading styles: **conservative** and **aggressive**. While conservative traders tend to take little to medium amount of risk, aggressive traders are risk-averse and tend to take more risks in trading. Generally, each trader falls into one of these two groups. In this chapter, we'll learn how to prepare, execute, and manage trades under these two different trade approaches.

1. Conservative Trading Style

You might think that conservative trading doesn't sound exciting, but playing it safe and small is never a bad thing, especially for the traders who have just dipped their toes in the treading world. I understand we all want to make money quickly, and that's all great, but I made all my profits by grinding my way up from a $1,000 account. Believe me when I say I didn't make money fast. It took me years of grind to get up to the level I always wanted to be at. I hope to shorten that learning curve for you based on my experience.

Conservative trading means that you'll be trading not more than 10 trades per month. Simple as that.

Best Waves To Trade

Within the Motive Phase, we are going to trade Waves 1 and 3 only. Within the Corrective Phase, the only tradable wave is Wave C if we are in a Zig-Zag formation.

Trade with the Trend

For conservative trades, you must trade in the direction of the larger trend!

- **Example #1** – You've found three waves on the EUR/USD that climb on the 1-hour chart, and the 4-hour timeframe is showing a bullish trend. Your theory is valid.

- **Example #2** – You've found five waves on the GBP/USD that climb on the 1-hour chart, and the 4-hour timeframe is bearish. Your theory is invalid.

Minimum Risk Reward

The minimum R/R that you should consider is 1:3 (Example: 30-pip stop vs 90-pip target).

Maximum Risk Per Trade

For accounts below $10,000: risk 2%. For bigger accounts: risk 1%.

These might at first appear to be small. However, with a minimum R/R of 1:3, we are aiming at either a 6% or 3% win per trade.

Best Timeframe?

For this type of trading, the best timeframes to use are 1-hour (1H), 4-hour (4H), or Daily (1D).

How To Trade Impulsive Wave #3

Pre-Trade Requirements

The larger trend needs to be Bullish/Bearish (4H or 1D)

Wave 1 needs to have 5 smaller sub-waves that respect the rules of the Motive Phase.

Optional Requirement

Between sub-waves 3 and 5, you should be able to see divergence on the RSI.

Conservative Entry for Wave #3

For the entry point, we place our pending BUY/SELL at the 50% Fibonacci retracement level of Impulsive Wave 1.

Image 58

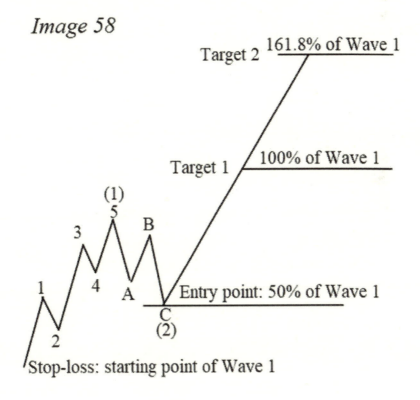

79

Conservative Stop for Wave #3

For the stop-loss, use the starting point of Wave 1 (Wave 2 can't break the start of Wave 1, otherwise, our setup would be invalid).

Conservative Exit for Wave #3

For targets, use the 100% and 161.8% extensions of Wave 1 as projected from the end of Wave 2.

Tips For Trading Wave 3

Move the stop to the break-even point (entry point) once the first target (100%) is reached.

Monitor how many sub-waves you have in Wave 3 once your trade's reached the first target. If there are already five waves in Wave 3, close the entire trade.

How To Trade Impulsive Wave #5

Pre-Trade Requirements

The larger trend needs to be Bullish/Bearish (4H or 1D). Wave 3 needs to have 5 smaller sub-waves. Wave 3 needs to test the 161.8% extension of Wave 1.

Optional Requirement

Between sub-waves 3 and 5, you should be able to see divergence on the RSI.

Conservative Entry for Wave #5

For the entry point, we are going to place our pending BUY/SELL at the 38.2% Fibonacci retracement level of Impulsive Wave 3. (Unless Wave 3 is an extended wave, we use the 23.6% level for entry).

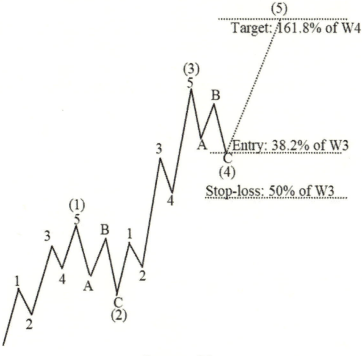

Image 59

Conservative Stop for Wave #5

For the stop-loss, use the 50.0% Fibonacci retracement level of Impulsive Wave 3.

Conservative Exit for Wave #5

For targets, use the inverse 161.8% level of Wave 4.

Move the stop to the break-even point once the price breaks above the end of Wave 3.

How to Trade Corrective Wave C

Pre-Trade Requirements

The larger trend needs to be Bearish/Bullish (4H or 1D). Wave A needs to have 5 smaller sub-waves.

Optional Requirement

Between sub-waves 3 and 5 you should be able to see divergence on the RSI.

Conservative Entry for Wave C

For the entry point, place a pending BUY/SELL at the 50% Fibonacci retracement level of Impulsive Wave A.

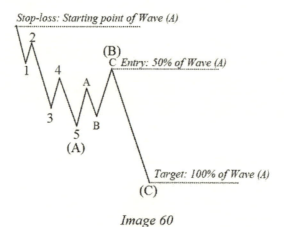

Image 60

Conservative Stop for Wave C

For the stop-loss, use the starting point of Wave A.

Conservative Exit for Wave C

For the targets, we use a 100% extension of Wave A projected from the end of Wave B.

Tips For Trading Wave C

Move the stop to the break-even point once the price breaks below the end of Wave A.

2. Aggressive Trading Style

Aggressive Trading is designed for traders who want high returns in a short period of time. Some traders are risk-takers by nature. They tend to take action more with the hope of grasping desired results in less time. In aggressive trading, you can expect to take 2 to 3 trades per day, but don't forget to limit yourself when necessary. Once you are satisfied with your profit for the day, just move away from your trading desk and spend time doing other activities (the point is to not end up handing all your gains back over to your broker).

Best Waves to Trade?

Within the Motive Phase, we are going to trade Waves 1 and 3. Within the Corrective Phase, the only tradable wave is Wave C unless we are in a Zig-Zag correction.

Trade with the Trend?

In aggressive trading, you can ignore trading with the trend, but try to adopt this method around 50% of the time only. For example, say you take 10 trades, then a maximum of 5 is allowed to be against the trend.

- **Example #1** - You found three waves on the GBP/USD that climb on the 1H chart, while the 4H timeframe is showing a bullish trend. The trade setup is valid.

- **Example #2** - You found five waves on the CAD/JPY that climb on the 1H chart, and the 4H timeframe is bearish. The trade setup is invalid.

Minimum Risk Reward

The minimum R/R that you should consider is 1:2 (for example 20-point stop vs 40-point target).

Maximum Risk per Trade?

For accounts below $10,000: risk 3-4%. For accounts from $10,000: risk 2%.

Best Timeframe?

For this type of trading, the best timeframes are the 15-minute (15min) and 30-minute (30min).

How To Trade Impulsive Wave #3

Pre-Trade Requirements

Wave 1 needs to have 5 smaller sub-waves that respect the rules of the Motive Phase.

Optional Requirement

Between sub-waves 3 and 5 you should be able to see divergence on the RSI.

Aggressive Entry for Wave #3

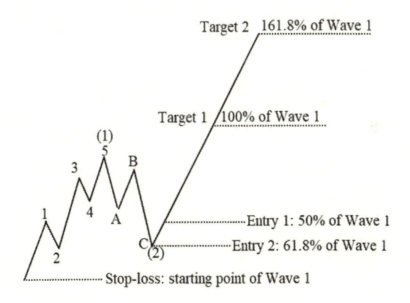

Image 61

For the entry point, place two pending orders to BUY/SELL at the 50% and 61.8% Fibonacci retracement levels of Impulsive Wave 1.

Aggressive Stop for Wave #3

To decide the stop-loss for both pending orders use the starting point of Wave 1.

Aggressive Exit for Wave #3

For the targets, we use the 100% and 161.8% extensions of Wave 1 projected from the end of Wave 2.

Tips For Trading Wave 3

- Move the stop to the break-even point once the first target (100%) is reached.

- Check how many sub-waves you have in Wave 3 once you reach the first target. If there have been five waves, close the entire trade.

How To Trade Impulsive Wave #5

Pre-Trade Requirements

Wave 3 needs to have 5 smaller sub-waves and to test the 161.8% extension level of Wave 1.

Optional Requirement

Between sub-waves 3 and 5, you should be able to see divergence on the RSI.

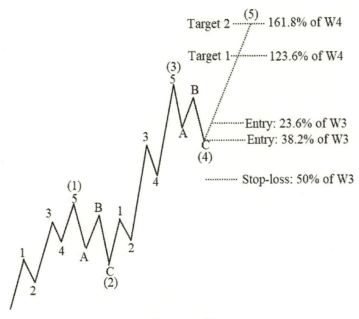

Image 62

For the entry point, place two pending orders to BUY/SELL at the 23.6% and 38.2% Fibonacci retracement levels of Impulsive Wave 3.

Aggressive Stop for Wave #5

Place the stop-loss for both pending orders at the 50.0% Fibonacci retracement level of Impulsive Wave 3.

Aggressive Exit for Wave #5

For the targets, use the inverse of 123.6% and 161.8% levels of Wave 4.

Move the stop to the break-even point once the price breaks above the end of Wave 3.

How To Trade Corrective Wave C

Pre-Trade Requirements

Before the Corrective Phase, we need to have a complete five-wave move (the Motive Phase). Moreover, Wave A needs to have 5 smaller sub-waves.

Optional Requirement

Between sub-waves 3 and 5, you should be able to see divergence on the RSI.

Aggressive Entry for Wave C

For the entry point, place two pending orders to BUY/SELL at the 50% and 61.8% Fibonacci retracement levels of Impulsive Wave A.

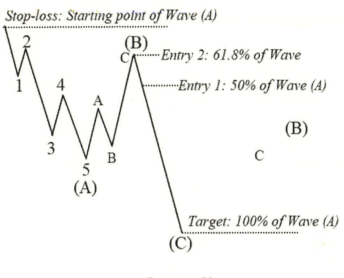

Image 63

Aggressive Stop for Wave C

For the stop-loss for both pending orders, use the starting point of Wave A.

Tips For Trading Wave C

Move the stop to the break-even point once the price breaks above the end of Wave A.

Aggressive Exit for Wave C

For our trading target, use the 100% extension of Wave A projected from the end of Wave B.

So, we've gone through different methods of preparing, identifying, executing, and managing trade in connection with different waves and patterns in the Elliott cycle. There are some differences in the way we set our entries, stop-losses, and profit targets. Successful trading requires a clear determination of whether you are a conservative or aggressive trader, and a consistent application of the rules and techniques presented. In the next chapter, we'll see how these rules and guidelines are applied in a lot of trade examples using both conservative and aggressive trading methods.

Example #1 - Aggressive Buy Trade USD/CHF

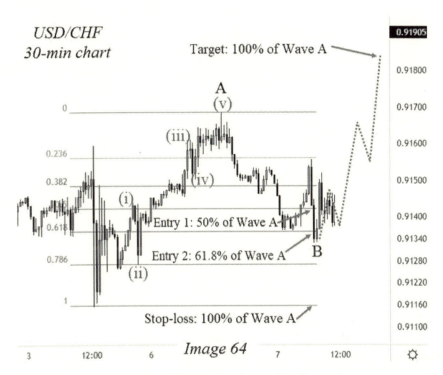

Image 64

In this example, the USD/CHF pair showed a five-sub-wave move in Wave A. As we know, the only type of correction resulting from this kind of Wave A is the Zig-Zag, hence we trade Wave C. Moreover, we are using a smaller timeframe (less than a 1Hr), therefore an aggressive approach is adopted.

- For entry points, we use the 50% & 61.8% retracement levels of Wave A.

- For the stop-loss, we use the starting level of Wave A.

- For the target, we use the 100% extension level of Wave A projected from the end of Wave B.

Image 65

Example #2 - Aggressive Sell Trade USD/CAD

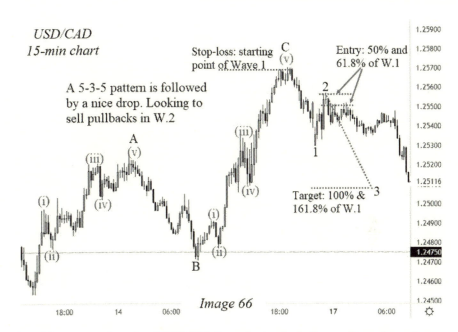

Image 66

In this example, the USD/CAD pair traded for a few days in an upward trend. On the chart, we can see that the movement was corrective in nature. We had three waves in total that looked like a Zig-Zag. After a strong, sharp drop in the price, we started to watch for a potential sell trade.

- For entry points, we use the 50% & 61.8% retracement levels of Wave 1.

- For the stop-loss, we use the start of Wave 1.

- For the targets, we use the 100% and 161.8% extensions of Wave 1 projected from the end of Wave 2.

Image 67

As you can see on the second chart, our two targets were reached quickly.

Example #3 - Aggressive Buy Trade EUR/AUD

Image 68

In this example, a nice five-wave bearish move had developed on the EURNZD pair, followed by a higher spike that looks impulsive. Hence, we expect another Zig-Zag correction. Although we are on the 1H chart, Wave C is our target. I would use an aggressive approach here because we are trading against the trend.

- For entry points, we use the 50% and 61.8% retracement levels of Wave A.

- For our stop-loss, we use the start of Wave A.

- For the target, we use the 100% extension of Wave A projected from the end of Wave B.

As you can see in the image below, after a few hours, the target was reached.

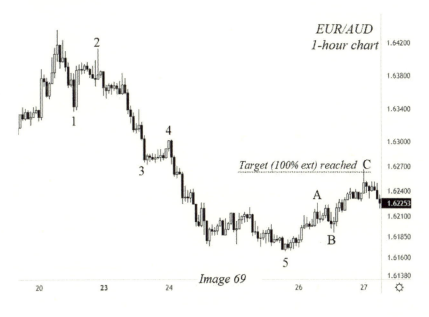

Image 69

95

Example #4 - Conservative Buy Trade USD/MXN

Image 70

The USD/MXN had strong ascending movement, and from the swing low we only had three waves, of which Wave 3 was much stronger than Wave 1. We use Wave 4's pullback to enter a long position.

- For the entry point, we use the 23.6% retracement level of Wave 3.

- For the stop-loss, we use the 50% retracement level of Wave 3.

- For the target, we use the inverse 161.8% level of Wave 4.

Image 71

Although the trade took some time to play out, we didn't have any problems along the way and finally reached our target.

Example #5 - Conservative Sell Trade USD/JPY

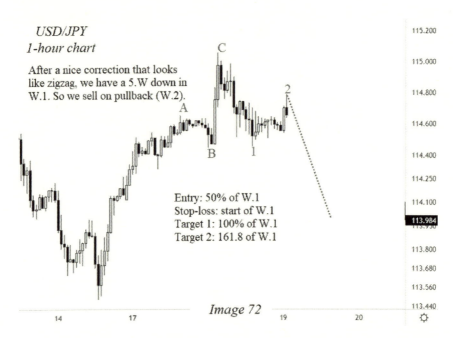

Image 72

In this example, the USD/JPY chart had an interesting 3 bullish waves that appear as a simple A-B-C type. Hence, we expect the next 5 downward waves. Now, even if you don't know the larger count, you can tell yourself that this is either the end of Wave 1 or Wave A. In both cases, you are going to get a pullback that will be a good place to sell.

- For entry points, we use the 50% & 61.8% retracement levels of Wave 1.

- For the stop-loss, we use the start of Wave 1.

- For the target, we use the 100% extension of Wave 1 projected from the end of Wave 2.

Once again, our targets were eventually reached after some swing ups and downs.

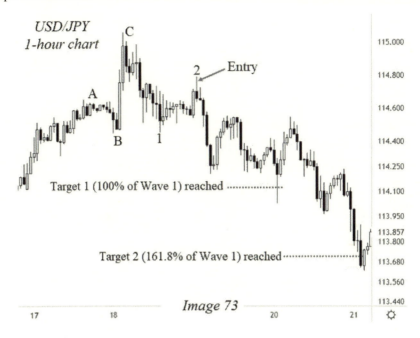

Image 73

Example #6 - Conservative Buy Trade USD/CAD

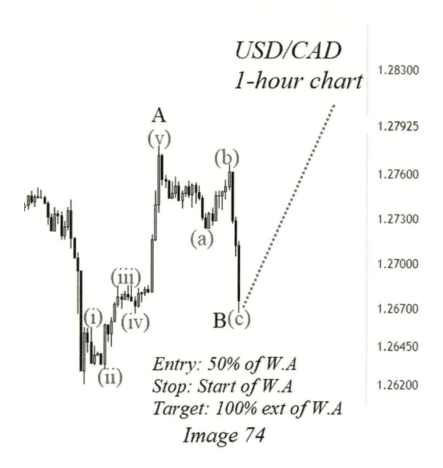

USD/CAD
1-hour chart

1.28300

1.27925

1.27600

1.27300

1.27000

1.26700

1.26450

1.26200

A
(v)

(b)

(a)

(iii)

(i)

(iv)

(ii)

B(c)

Entry: 50% of W.A
Stop: Start of W.A
Target: 100% ext of W.A

Image 74

In this example, we see that the USD/CAD larger trend is definitely up. After a nice amount of downward movement, we finally spot a decent five-wave move to the upside. Hence, we are in a position to go long (buy) after a reliable correction (Wave B).

- For the entry point, we use the 50% retracement level of Wave A.

- For the stop-loss, we use the start of Wave A.

- For the target, we use the 100% extension of Wave A projected from the end of Wave B.

Image 75

After around two days, our targets were reached using the conservative method.

Example #7 - Aggressive Sell Trade AUD/CAD

Image 78

On this AUD/CAD chart, we can see a nice upward trend that is composed of five waves in the direction of the larger trend. Using our method, we can expect at least a three-wave movement in the opposite direction. After waiting for the first leg to complete, we watch for Wave B to determine our trade positions.

- For entry points, we use the 50% & 61.8% retracement levels of Wave A.

- For the stop-loss, we use the start of Wave A.

- For the target, we use the 100% extension of Wave A projected from the end of Wave B.

Once again, both of our entry targets were filled promptly.

AUD/CAD
15-min chart

B

0
0.236
0.382
0.5
0.618
0.786

A

Target reached

1.618

C

0.92250
0.92200
0.92150
0.92100
0.92089
0.92050
0.92000
0.91950
0.91890
0.91830
0.91770
0.91710
0.91660
0.91610
0.91560

12:00   18:00   21   06:00

Image 79

On the second chart, we can see that our target for Wave C was also reached quite quickly.

CONCLUSION

So, we've come to the end of this book.

First of all, I would personally like to congratulate you on deciding to improve your trading with my assistance. If you are reading this section, you are one step closer to pushing your trading to the next level.

Trading has never been easy to all of us. Yet, the fact is that each trader can improve their trading results by constantly practicing and improving the way they read market fluctuations. Trading is not about how much you earn in one day, one month, or one year. It is about whether you are developing the right thoughts and acting the right way. After all, trading is all about constructive actions repeated again, and again, and again. Believe in yourself, and keep moving forward with the help of powerful Elliott Wave techniques presented in this book.

Finally, if you find you have learned something useful via this book, please leave a few kind words in the review section. I would be very grateful to you.

Happy trading!

Steve Sinclair

In this Appendix, we'll show how to draw Fibonacci retracements and expansions on tradingview.com.

1. Drawing Fibonacci retracements

- Select the Fib Retracement Tool from the drop-down menu on the left side of the trading screen.

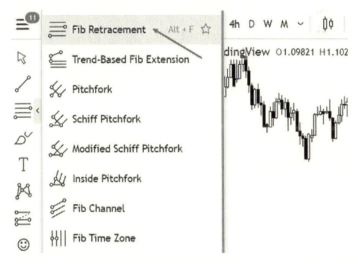

- Next, you click on the starting point of the swing (the swing high in a downtrend, and swing low in an uptrend), move (don't hold) it to the ending point of the swing (swing low in a downtrend and swing high in an uptrend). Fibonacci retracement levels will automatically appear on the chart.

In this picture, the 1.618 line is the inverse 161.8% level that we're mentioned a few times in this book. However, this level is not automatically set in the Fib retracements tool.

- To insert it, click on any available retracement level on the chart to select, then continue to right-click on that level, and choose the "setting" at the end of the drop-down menu. A new window will open as in the following picture.

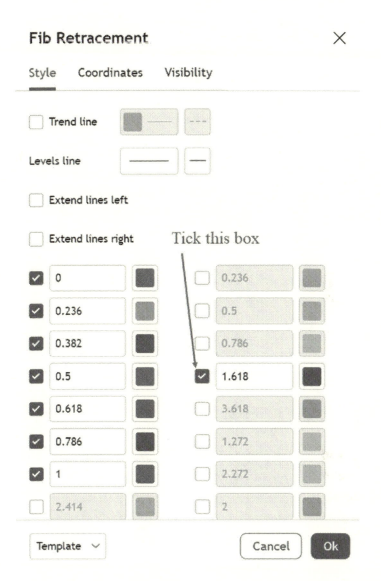

- Simply tick an additional 1.618 box, then click "ok", and done. (You can add as many levels as you want).

2. Drawing Fibonacci expansions

- First, you choose the Fib expansions on the menu at the left hand of the tradingview screen.

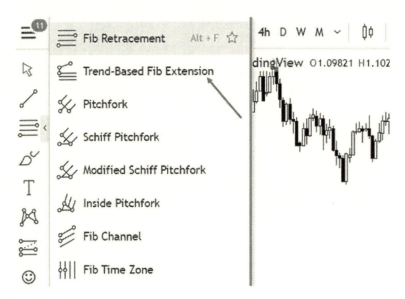

- Draw the retracement. There are three clicks you'll need to make. First, you make one left-click at the start of the swing (the swing low in the uptrend example below). Then, move the cursor to the end of the swing (the swing high) and make another left-click. Finally, continue to move the cursor to the end of the next wave (the corrective wave) and make the final click. Now you have complete Fibs expansion levels drawn on the chart. Again, you can add some other levels to the chart by visiting the setting menu.

Swing high
(second click)

0.786

0.618

0.5

0.382

0.236

Third click

0

Swing low (first click)

109

Manufactured by Amazon.ca
Bolton, ON